KAEYAHUES

(SHADES OF A MONSOON FLOWER)

Tejas Bais 'Aagneya'

Made with ❤ on the Notion Press Platform

www.notionpress.com

Contents

2. Self-Reflection & Identity: The Mirror Within

3. Nature & Metaphors: Whispers of the Earth

4. Philosophy & Society: The Mind's Battlefield

5. Poetry on Poetry: The Poet's Soul

Preface

In law, it is said that **"Denial is the best defence."** We all deny the situation and the forthcoming scenarios that life, in all its audacity, throws our way. Maybe we all want to let go of the things that disrupt the natural and dear flows of our lives, and yet we are mesmerized by the urge to hold onto them. I, too, am denying the fact that my beloved Autumn lasted only nine surreal nights, and as the dawn of life runs by, all dreams are forgotten in the atonement of those nights.

However, only in such denial does one become more than ordinary. It is possible to live life to the fullest in every minute and every second, for it is the ephemerality of those transcendent moments that nurtures the fortunes in our lives.

The poems present here stand as witnesses to the testament of changing times, as seen by poets and people alike. The emotion of longing is so personal, yet so universal, that everyone can relate to it. These poems speak of an emotion so crowded, yet lonely, that the dwellers of the midnight storm can feel its essence—yet it remains presentable and mysterious to those who seek joy. But there are other expressions which are always in periphery to the generous stories of union and separation, and in all romanticism, there is escape from the larger gravity of truth. The truth about the tantrums of love and lust, the godly and unjust, the splendour of efforts and time's rust, there are larger truths too. It is only my mere expression and exploration to understand where I stand in all the stories of life.

I thus hand you over these poems and some poetic stories.

Acknowledgement

Deepest gratitude to all who stood by me and endured the mood swings of a self-proclaimed newbie poet.

To my friends and family—your faith and honest feedback shaped this book (and saved it from disaster more than once, though who's to say another isn't lurking?).

To her (the eternal muse)—obsession with an idea can be a great motivator, sometimes the only one.

And to those who believed in me when I couldn't—this book is yours too… but the royalties? Well, that depends on whether anyone actually buys *and* reads it!

But let's be honest—this whole thing is mostly a formality, isn't it?

LOVE & LONGING: ECHOES OF THE HEART

I Was Sitting Beside Neruda

The dew drops fell, the lights glimmered, the distance
shivered.
Hopes plundered the soul all night.
The Constitution ridiculed the rights.
The night turned pale green, the moon yellow, and the sun
all white.
Ah... and I simply kept waiting.

I was sitting beside Neruda when he wrote the saddest of all
lines tonight.
I was cutting the rope of a gloomy kite,
The kite that once flew in your majestic skies,
That shivered in your winds, that halted for your glimpse,
And, in your adornment, leaped and rose.

Ah... I simply kept waiting, and
I found that the verses of the past are all lies.
It is very much present now—the longing, the pain, the hope...
everything.

I was watching Neruda when he wrote the saddest of all
lines tonight.
I copied him all my life, all the trivial things he must have
done

For the song unsung,
For the platonic revolution you call yours, mine, or a soul sublime.
I was Neruda once when he wrote the saddest of all lines tonight.

Ah... and I simply kept waiting...
For the memories to trifle you with the same agony,
Besides all revolutions of heart and bane.

I was sitting beside Neruda when he wrote the saddest of all lines tonight.
Ah... and I simply kept waiting for the poem to be completed once and for all.

Why don't you come for once—not for me, not for my soul to find peace, but for Neruda... for he loved you, and sometimes you loved him too.
I plead that a poet's guilt is impatience; come once, if redemption is true.

Ah... waiting and waiting... I am still sitting beside Neruda when he is writing the saddest of all lines tonight.
"I loved her, and sometimes she loved me too."

For story's sake, for creation's sake, if once in the world all lies are true.

What Fulfilled Promises Do!

Roses murmured, *"Please don't pluck us for the sake of your promises."*
Oh humans, do you really take your promises seriously?
Do you fulfil them? —they asked tenderly, in their loving demeanour.

But then, you were standing in front of me, with a sparkled face, sharp eyes, and roaring lips, your skin radiating with rainbows, as if the rain had adorned you with a thousand colours.

How could I have not plucked them to share their beauty with you?
But they were loving flowers too, and they would wither, as promises do.

And you are—you are shades of the monsoon flower (Kaeyahues), as they say,
Erupting with a thousand emotions and making me feel all of them.
You were a flower—more beautiful, more fragrant, more surreal...
I couldn't pluck flowers for you...

Just stare into my eyes, and you will see what fulfilled promises do.

For now, I bid adieu...

Monsoon Flower

Perhaps every story has its end, to not truly end but to resurface in spirals, in all metaphors of life.

Yesterday, the monsoons came, refreshing all the withered escapes of a long dune of ephemeral heat, dulcet and laughing at her own deeds. The monsoon came correcting me, laughing at the confusion of a poet, a poet who in his poem wrote "moon flower" instead of "monsoon flower." The monsoon claimed that it is her, it is her alone that lays claim to the metaphors of my poem.

The moon is dim, fragile, and nonchalant, but I feel every word of yours and utter it in perpetuity. My rains own your words and they sing them, giving life and lessons to all who keep their heads up and feel.

But I am a night walker, I write and live in the refuge of night. But then it is true, isn't it?

Why is the moon, not the rain, the supreme metaphor of my poetry?

Why does the moon seem so ordinary before the rain? Perhaps because the rain washes away my heritage, my words—

Even under the shadow of the moon, the rain erases them.

The moon merely watches my despair, while the rain nurtures creation.
The rain births flowers that will one day turn into trees,
So that in their shade, others may find peace, even if for a moment.
Maybe there must be some other reason too.

Basket Full of Wishes

In a basket once, I collected all my wishes for you:
The light hope for your bright future, the strong resolve to
be together, and the reverence that I have for you.
I wished that you would too fill the basket with all promises
of shared existence,
But you threw the basket away, all the wishes that were for
you.

Why? I can't even ask you the reason. Was that really you?
Even after the months, we changed roads—you cross my
heart a million times,
And I sob a thousand times for loving you.

And then, a poet too was at my door, talking about estranged
love,
Talking of the passion to keep it and try for it till the last breath.
He found solace in my pain; I don't know when he fell for me,
But I closed his doors too... for I collected all wishes for you...

How could you? How could you?

Maybe I Pleaded with All My Heart

Maybe I pleaded with all my heart that God acquit me of all
attachments that I had with my desires and aspirations.
Maybe I pleaded with all my heart that He give me relief
from friendship and company, covered in the veil of His love.

My case was the toughest of its time, a messy one.
I begged with all my heart that I wouldn't abscond, I wouldn't
run.
I had to convince a child under 7 holding a gun,
Innocent and betrayed by the treachery and cruelty of life,
A *doli incapax*, unable to understand the nature of his crime.
And it was all voluntary, for I was the one wanting to get hurt,
But I too feared getting wounded by the shot,
And it was *Volanti non fit injuria*, where relief was impossible,
for I was the one signing for the hurt.

I thought I may not be heard and justice would be denied,
But maybe He is there, and all destinies are justified.
I was not sure that He would ever apply the principle of
Natural Justice to my case—*Audi Alteram Partem*, let the
other side be heard.

But, to my surprise, in His serene presence, He heard my
plea, the emotions, and every word.
And I was granted relief...

Maybe I pleaded with all my heart,
Or maybe He was kind to me...
I rest my feelings and faith in You, Your Lordship.

Poet Met Nastenka

Once a poet met a lover, a poet herself, sitting alone at a crowded railway station in Nizamuddin.

She was beautifully gloomy that day, as if the moon were shining in all its luminance, yet dark and shattered.

She was murmuring poetry of longing, so serene and fascinating that I couldn't help but be bewitched by it. I was a dreamer, and she was Nastenka, and it was all a white night.

Where delusion, dream, and reality intermingled with fate and destiny.

She was waiting for the story, or perhaps she kept waiting enough to end it.
And she was the betrayal of the Lord, mourning for it.

She carved the ink of love on her heart and gave all to the ounce of love she thought was hers.

She cried to the woods, and those heartless woods couldn't even answer her once.

I asked her, "Where were you before, poet, when the woods were reaching out to you for words, screaming metaphorically?

When you had the power to engulf everything with words, what were you doing with silence?"

She replied, "I was mad in love, or madly in love, when you screamed for me.
My dear, what are you? You seek revenge on me. What are you, my lover?

If I hadn't known my ill fate of living and entering hell's gate, I would have said yes. But poets are meant to live alone and in solitude."

So I said, "I am a poet seeking stories of passion and suffering. You know, once I lost the precious one ring."

And it was a great conversation, you know, like strangers do with their hearts free. I don't know why she thanked me. Goodbyes are okay, but she cursed me, saying that one day I would meet the right person whom I would love the most. The stories are always of the ifs and almosts.

And thus,
The Dreamer met Nastenka again in the white nights, where truth faded in the fog of dreams.
This time, Nastenka was different than before, but the Dreamer dreamt, lingered, and in joy screamed.
The Dreamer told her about the dream he lived many times, where Nastenka left him for her love.
This time, Nastenka told him, "I say, those who think love is not exchanged are foolish. Women function in reciprocation. And sometimes pouring too. Some men, some women don't.

To not love because you bleed is stupid. Bleed. Love. That's what exists eternally. And I've said before as well, as of this lifetime, all I have is faith."

The Dreamer was a poet too, writing letters was his flu. He knew everything and yet said,
"The ache... you know, the ache that keeps you moving, the one that causes you pain and you still laugh with it. I know it will happen, it is inevitable, and perhaps it shouldn't happen again. I don't want to live the cycles of life and death all over again when I know the ill fates."

And she smartly replied, "The Dreamer is perhaps not the dreamer with all the 'buts' and 'ifs'.
A life with her in 'buts' and 'ifs' still would be a gift.
But you know the story, don't you, Nastenka?
You closed your gates for everyone, for the Dreamer too.
And you took a promise from him that the night would be the last, the last of it.
And it was yet again four nights of a dreamer who lived through inevitable pain.
You left with the dew of the dawn, with the good enough dream of the night where the dreamer mourns.
'Your hand is cold, mine burns like fire. How blind you are, Nastenka!'"

And all I had again was the last letter for you with me.
Nastenka, you know what I feel unhappy about the most?
It's that I never wanted to be loved, but I hated that you don't want to be loved by me. Nights hurt!

What was my fault, Nastenka, that I met you on the bridge where you were, longing for someone's return?
What was my fault when I wrote you poems and letters in admiration?
Speak, O Lord of words, why am I being punished with the silence of words? Why?
Why, Nastenka? Why? For I write dreams, I live them, or is it the Muse I had the audacity to fall for?

Bewitched by the Charms

Every night, you bewitch me with your poetic charms—
I long to be loved by you, to be held in your arms.

Don't be anything for me,
For once I have held you, you won't be free.
Your lips will seek freedom, yet your hands will be my slaves,
And my body will navigate the curves and caves.

Don't be anything for me,
I desire you, poetess—your art, your soul.

Every night, you take me to your soothing deserts,
Where blood spills and turns to heaven for wanderers to seek
and thrive.
How can one be so serene and desirable?
As the desert is—for time immemorial.

I cover you over my head,
As shepherds do when they wander in search of pastures of
life.
I graze upon the altar of your ruins,
And wonder at the twilight of your eyes.

Your Presence

It was pinnacle of thought when you were here, talking about almost everything; life, death, love and sacrifice.

And I couldn't help myself thinking of adorning your hairs with Gajra for they are you in every lifetime creating an eternal image of your beloved.

I couldn't help myself distancing from a thought of taking your hand for a moment and staring the lines on your palms and slowly kissing it.

Only to erase what might have been written about me there.

Dearest, it is not the fear that drives me here, it is the fever that has entangled my throat to keep singing for you...even if there is a silence.

Sometimes you are a muse, sometimes a friend and other times a stranger...

And all of the above a creative danger.

The Ninth Note

You are the octave of my heart; the ninth note, your smile.
Every step of yours a band, every word, a style.
How is your language so serene, so simple to learn,
like the melody of breath and the blossom of the sun?
If you had spoken the toughest of languages,
I would have learned that too,
as the waves learn the language of the sea,
a language that sets them aloof, that sets them free.

But you speak... you speak the language of marbles,
the tranquil, noble marbles that adorn the Taj,
telling the story of a beggar who grieved his misery,
and of ephemeral love—Mumtaz.
But the marbles over the banks of the Yamuna
sing in a rhythm that transcends time.

You are the octave of my soul; the ninth note, your smile—
it doesn't even need to rhyme.
Of all the souls, the kind tune of them, I loved once,
and for that, I am blessed.
For I now sing beyond the octaves that strive and struggle,
not for less, but for more.
I can only say, beyond realms of music, philosophy, and
understanding,

that even a lifetime is not enough to fathom your existence.
Only I can harp the melody of you,
for you are the octave of my heart,
the soul; the ninth note, your smile.

The Warmth in Your Words

The warmth you have in your words,

I feel the same in your lament hugs,

For I have never known the soul is more beautiful than carnal thoughts,

Let alone the thought win and body rot,

Yet my lips despise me for claiming you,

It is a new era for me too,

I claim that you are muse to me tonight,

I am asking, I have that right?

The Eyes of Yours

The gazelle eyes of yours stared at me in astonishment,
As if I were guilty of bewildering them.
That was the first instance poetry spoke through me—
In every minuscule space and every lingering dot,
Where desire ended, and something unknown began.

In the seclusion of the divide,
Where the sea tampered with the moon's shine,
Where mere words rhymed with the divine,
It flowed through me.

And it was not love, it was never meant to be.
It was simply your existence, dear—
Your existence that birthed poems of longing and passion.

All That My Heart Was

All that my heart was—without fear.
I was deaf with eyes and blind with ears,
For I had not heard the blinding scream of unuttered chatters.
And for that, only an image remains—a memory, a voice;
now, nothing matters.

My poems are all gone, missing or torn,
For I have always turned to them with a blind eye,
For I have always unwelcomed hellos and hurriedly said
goodbye.

Now, all that my heart screams—I can't hear.
I can't see where my hands are, what am I writing.
Now, all my heart does is scream—a lot,
An uncanny shout that I myself can't hear,
And yet, all I have is shivering fear.

Yet, I remain grateful for my hands, that I can wipe my tears.
And though my heart—like myself—remained deaf with
eyes and blind with ears,
All that they can sense is her ever-joyful cheer.

A Thousand Things

The unphased, unfocused, unethical life I stride upon
Lies hopeless in the lament of perpetual cycles—
Of paths and impasses intertwined.

Then I try to write, to set right
The ardent animus of every gaze.

But then—

A thousand words I wrote,
A thousand words I erased.
A thousand eyes ignored,
A thousand eyes gazed.
A thousand voices murmured,
A thousand voices raised.
A thousand times I lived,
A thousand times I razed.

And in a thousand lifetimes,
You looked upon me as man looks upon the stars,
Claiming them as his own.

Yet in all those thousand times,
I was the writer, writing for you—
And the universe read along with you.

A thousand times over, you see—
In a thousand agonies, I live.
And I think I shall live forever,
Until you read me.

A Poem Is Enough to Make Her Remember or Not?

Some days, a poem is enough to make her remember,

The unforgettable vows, the midnight talks and never-ending walks,

Some days it's hard to make her remember anything,

As if all those moments we cherished are nothing,

Some days she doesn't remember anything at all,

Yes, it's unbelievable to think for any feeling to fall,

Some days, I don't even try to make her remember anything,

I have learnt my lesson and with tears, I say, "Oh, it's nothing".

Some days, out of my rage, I pen down all the thoughts,

I curse every human, and bless that rots,

Some days, to make her remember everything, I write that all the rulers are fake,

And all the lives are at stake,

With all the hidden symbols of love and rage inside,

I express the idea, the idea to hide,

Some days, I can't make her remember anything,

Oh it's good that I can't write nothing,

Nothing, no one remembers her, Why should I suffer,

Some days, it's just a thought,

Some days, maybe, perhaps, let it be

Medical Negligence

"Doctors... I hate their kind," said he, and a friend fondly asked, "Why?"

"Ah, they always make me remember that illness exists. Everyone would have to suffer pain anyhow, but no one would know the kind of it, without doctors... but they don't treat love, which is a serious mental illness."

"But you can't blame them," friend rebutted, "Love is not a disease."

"And yet, why does it hurt?"

"That is a different matter. What have doctors done to you?"

"They escalated my pain out of negligence," said he, and then no further question remained.

And again, my overused brain started to think of all the possibilities and circumstances arising out of mere words... words that never conveyed true meaning. I want her to talk, and at the same time, I want her to ignore my plea... Oh, how great is the drama of the heart, the push and pull of expectations, action and reaction of life. My heart wants her to answer me immediately, without a thought, but doesn't want her to reply, avoiding her work, her leisure, her life. Great is such frustration, great is such drama, the reincarnation and rebirths of such circumstances, and so is the salvation out of the answer.

She's Popping Out of My Head

She's still inside my head, popping out every time when I
see a toddler laugh on the gaze of life,

She freezes me out with her full smile.

Those winter shaken lips of hers splendid on a cotton wine,

she is still inside my head like unwind time.

The smell of her long oily hairs, of which she told me that
she left washing them,

cause she was in hurry, ah reason of which is still only a
ridicule to me.

She is still very much inside my head, popping out every time

I try to hold the hand of the reality. Is she no longer here or
it's just my head?

Let it be, strange one, you know? She is still inside my head,
and silent and stern beside a harrowing bed.

Doctor! Please take her out! Help me with it or it's just
incurable growing something?

All the Ages Are Lost

All the ages are lost in your pursuit, beloved.

The grandeur of mosques and temples lost in your solace and there are now ruins of once splendid prayers for you.

For your seekers, your devotees sought permanence in the ephemerality of creation. Beloved, now I know that it I have to want, I have to wish the same as God has drawn the web of fates for me. So, I have you? That's the question for life, beloved; strangest of the question.

Her Eyes Bewilder

Your eyes bewilder the existence of Godly creation,

I claim that you are His song, His expression.

When you crave the lips of your desire,

I am open to the thoughts that you inspire.

You are words, dear—the words that lay claim

On the very lips of silence.

You are not someone to be pleased in vile chains.

The serene eyes shatter and pierce deeper into the soul,

For she craves more.

She forbids the tantrums of even the darkest forelore.

Her desire echoes the visceral glimpse of the eclipse's night,

She is beauty, transcended in pure white.

But when she descends into the carnal rage of her desired form,

She is the law of the land, the sacred norm.

I can only adorn you with words, Muse,

Yet someday, your poems will make me desire you

As a primordial being—one who dies and lives within your words.

Silence in the Court

"I am tarnished by the thought of you. Please leave my mind, my heart and soul. I no longer cherish your memories; they are burden for me. Please leave me alone" He begged to her and still she remained silent, said nothing on his pain as she has done before. She is no cruel person, but he envied her joy; as the most sadistic person desire, he too desire the joy of being close to happiness herself. But in that very happiness lies the pain of wanting more and getting nothing. He tried to remain close to her only to remain distant. He even tried to stay silent with her, ignore her. But in his ignorance to he use to think," I won't talk to her but I can't live without talking about her." So he does and atlast after the ammends he stated his conversation back, he got his joy back. But everything was illusion and he hated that he loved her and decided to remain silent and thus his soul screamed to his joy, silence. He was so naive but in love so grave and yet love was nothing but silence.... silence. Silence in the court! Court where every matter of dispute is resolved by silence. Silence solves everything. Thus, seek silence... silence from your own voice. Want nothing, see nothing, feel nothing but silence.

Letter to the Stranger

Dearest Stranger,

Nights are dreadful. No one knows what can happen between the hours of the moon and the dawn and for those who consider the Strangers to be the guiding light of the nights, life is foggy for them.

I for the moment don't remember any word I spoke as if I was bewitched by the troublesome night and uttered ridicule in intoxication. I don't want to remember anything for I have lived every word, every sentence and every punctuation of yours. Yet, I have not lived enough.

Its not that I can't live without people or get hurt every time they leave, no one gets. We get hurt by our own expectations and dreams and my dream failed terribly for I wanted to follow your light in the dreaded night.

And after my fall when I slept, I had a constant dream where you came to wake me up, talked to me and said, we will remain forever as a silent conversation in the night. Ah…it was a sweetly terrible dream. I woke up and found myself lonely again.

Holding Onto and Letting Go

45

Whenever life tried to hold onto something it had to let it go,

Karna for the cries of a child held clay once, so strongly and with such reverence that the Goddess Earth cursed him, all in his misfortune.

When he held the head of his Guru in respect and took all the scathes from beetle's bite, yet again cursed for holding on despite.

When he held his Dharma in all honesty, his Dharma deceived him.

All misfortune come from holding on and all peace comes from letting go.

And we all know our destines of letting go and yet have the desire of holding on.

For we all are Karna, confused in the tantrums of life.

Echoes of Obsession

It's raging of thoughts, the whispering of bane,
Maybe this one is the heartbreak, maybe this one is the pain.
The anxious rhythm chilling insides, heart wrenching in lava beside,
The crying meadows of cheek—maybe the tears are the hilly peak.
My heart is struck with one commotion now,
What have you done, why, and how?
Was I really obsessed with her thoughts?
Did she really mean? that a lot?
Or was it only a stubbornness of a child
That, razed the peace, that raised the fire wild?
What must she have been feeling in all this mess?
Will she ever believe a friendly face?
But that poem, that poem she wrote was for me,
I could use it anywhere—I am free.
No, you are wrong here, poet—she is no machine as you are,
She wrote that with trust and pouring emotions.
But! No, listen to me, listen to me—
Sometimes things are perceived differently with different notions.
You were no one to display the evidence
Without evidence in an open court, without a reason.

Now you are destined to chase the thought—
It's your sentence, it's your prison.
Have I really lost that one?
Was I nothing—a no one?
Yes, you are no one, nothing to her.
Just forget her, just forget her, so that she won't suffer.
I promise, I will try my best,
But only there, there in my pilgrimage, will I find my rest.
How can someone be this idiotic?
A clear no is no, friend.
But it is my sole journey—you can only make amends.
You should really do something about your attachment and
obsession issues, poet.
You should.
I can't make you do things… You are hopeless.

The restless creek, the finer peak,
Who was he to write me down?
Ain't I a human? Not just a noun or pronoun.
He is a creep, selflessly obsessed with miserly thoughts.
He makes me uncomfortable, suffocate, and rot.
That internet creep posted a poem of mine,
And wrote a piece that doesn't even rhyme.
He was a bullshit freak,
A gatherer of words, his actions weak.
And I trusted him with the whispers of my heart.
I was such a fool; I thought I was smart.
He was a wolf in sheep's cowl.
That conversation was an accident, an ignorant foul.
And why in the world did I react to him?

Had he been so fanatical that I made a scream?
No, he is a creep—the internet one. I should not have trusted him.
It was, once again, a fantasy I wanted to live—a dark whim.
It's better that I blocked all his ways.
Now, I will be alone again, in solitude, with my healing days.

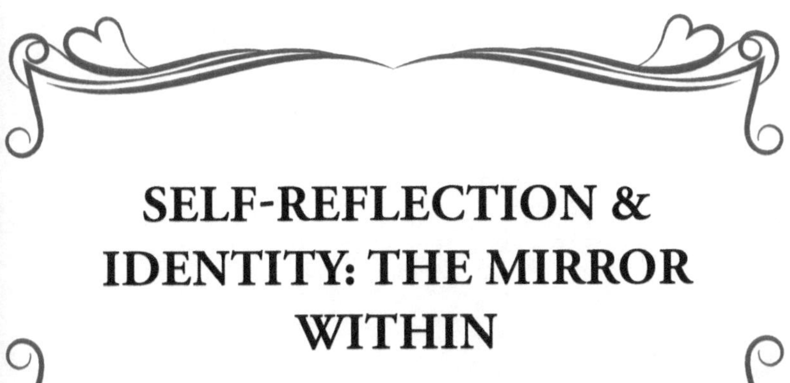

SELF-REFLECTION & IDENTITY: THE MIRROR WITHIN

Liberation

Now the signs of unworthiness have passed by,

I swirl in all bliss,

For his season passed, and I no longer remember him.

I made peace with myself,

And I am a free verse, writing and shaping my own destiny.

I am a proud poet, you see,

I will fly—not escape, nor flee.

Now the face of serenity has returned, and I am radiating a

thousand words.

I let go of all that mingled, hurt, and intertwined.

I am now all fit and fine.

I will write a million songs of my liberation,

For I am a force of devotion and faith,

Standing at liberation's gate.

Man Child

And then he imagined her as a woman
And cursed himself and her, "Ah… don't take the shape of my
dreams, lady, for God's sake, don't,"
And she kept reading the book for him.
But with a sudden burst of all pure and impure emotions,
with the joyous youthful urge, he knelt before his desire, yet
did nothing and left the room.
Well, he was standing not too close to her, so as not to distract
her from the devoted act of cooking, and not too distant, so
that he would miss the elegance of her while cooking.
But then he was a man-child, he could not control his urge to
read poetry for her.
"Hey," he took her name like the title of the poetry, and she
looked at him with unwavering charm, like a mother who
looks at her child.
And when he started reading, she reacted to the emotion of
every stanza, she laughed, she smiled, and she stayed silent for
a while until the cooker started whistling.

Beggar of Talk

"Don't speak to him; he is a beggar of talk. For all his life, he keeps begging people for a conversation, and in return, he spends all his fortunes and talent to keep them close. I have seen him barking like a dog at all those whom he considers thieves of his dear ones. He barks at them so that no one dares to take his loved ones away. But I have seen everyone fondling him and then leaving him to wander the gloomy streets, to starve and yearn. Don't speak to him, for he will hope again that someone will always be there for him. I don't want to see him suffer more; he has suffered enough. Please don't. Stay away from him for his sake."

How Are You?

Hey!
How are you?
Even if you don't answer,
Everything has its end, and it's ought to be true. I
understand that there is a long-standing queue,
Waiting patiently, quietly, or supposedly only for you.
You must answer them too.
Every call, though small,
Some might sprawl,
Waiting for you,
That is true, that is true...
I am one of them,
Of them all, sparing none,
Waiting for my turn,
To get answers to,
What the answers are, who knew.

It was a bad day without you,
All the world is a lie, but that is true.
And to the end of the day,
Hey, how are you?
If you can answer,
Like in all the poems of joy and misery,

I am waiting and in a hurry.
I can say that it was a bad day without you,
But time is waiting too,
All the world is a lie, but what is true is true,
It was a bad day without you.

How? I am too available, and you are not.
I will speak something, and you will just reply, "What?"
How can we just talk as friends,
When you are not free to make amends?
How?

Between spaces of just saying hello and hi, and then a
hesitant goodbye,
Between most of the silence,
This strips down a tiny little potion of hope,
Hope that when all the conversations end and nothing
remains,
We would just ask, "Hey, how are you?"

Are you seeing those beautiful lights there?
Where?
On those thorny trees, over there,
Are you seeing those couples? See how sweet they are looking.
Hmm,
Why is it so rushed today?
Oh, it's nothing, today is Christmas.
Like all the stories,
I came to know that it could be us.
You always asking curious questions,
I am answering them with the lame ones,

But as life goes on, the silence of life after a hasty rush,
And the manifestation of it, the silent us.
I have too much to write,
Maybe not tonight,
But someday,
I will tell my grandchildren that it was that night,
The night where I waited for a story to begin,
The story where losing is the win.
Let it be, it's Christmas,
And we are the distant us.
Let it be… for the conversation's sake.

How are you?
Asking you makes me happy too.
For all the good we shared over the years,
It's good that we both are sharing some happy tears.
Or nothing at all, it's good that we still are who we were.
But still, after all these years, it's a little hesitancy, a greater fear.
I have never told you that I was so into you.
That I remain myself a little too few.
It's good that I asked you once again, after all these years,
And honestly, it made me happy too.

Can We Talk If You Are Free

Some days, I really want to talk to someone, and some days, I
absolutely do not.
The world is a strange place; we breathe here, and here we rot.

Some days, I am absolutely a beggar for affection, and on
some days, I am a master of perfection.

Yet I feel that I should look and stare at beautiful things,
might embrace my own feelings.

Some days, I love what I hate, and some days, I look for
love which has not arrived yet.

Some days, every poem and story I wrote feels like a joke to me,
And on that day, I ask you, "Can we talk if you are free?"

I Dopped Out of a Life

I dropped out of a life that I thought was meant for
me, I prepared for it's entrance in early years of my life
where I could have, I would have done something else,
like drawing, sketching, playing all day long. But they
taught me, that I have to go to school, study and not sing
in my melody, my own song. I never had time to make
good friends you know, the type which are forever, but
I have some of them now. They will help in my venture
for a life that is beyond living. What do you think on
my dropping out of life which I thought will cater all my
fancies, where I would have been in best of the dresses,
would have experienced the ecstasy of life and the lore of
being successful. But now I think, ah...it isn't worth it. I
am dropping out of a life. You know, all these years what
they taught me of love was not real at all. Love as they
is not the way of life. I met a beloved once, I can claim
to meet her only once for the story purpose, she is all
that she claims not to be, she is both the war and peace,
the politician and the common, the oppressor and the
oppressed. And what they tell of the glorious story, it isn't
glorious at all. I met her again, as the ritual demand and

as if I found my peace. This is not the life I ever wanted,
that was the end of the conflict you know, the conclusion
of the story. Ah..I am dropping out of this life, I hardly
imagine now that I can live like this...with mundanity of
absolute nothingness.

My Inner Voice

And thus, the soul commanded, withdraw from every stage, every role you breathe in, you breathe with, or so shall die of despair for your soul less will to continue. I am at conflict with myself whether I am doing favour to others or they are doing favour to me by having me with them. Let it be, I am now feeling vengeful to a king who expressed his ungrateful displeasure when I jokingly said that the constitution of his kingdom is vague, being myself a writer of it and he said that his enemies will laugh at it. But to my hearts discontent now, I want to bring down that very kingdom of his, mine and others to ashes so that I can scream loudly, so loudly that the writer of all, the creator of all destines come to me and take my soul to hell where I shall laugh on my own sufferings. I shall drink my own tears, I shall hug my all fears for I am a soul, an earthly one and of them all a hellish tonne, My heart stays silent all the time and when in need and grief, it doesn't speak but tells me, run... run and run....

My Presence in Her Eyes

In serene breezes, in hefty haze,

I found your uncomfortable gaze.

It was my mere presence that was trifling all along,

That my letters were blasphemous throngs,

That my poems weren't making right any wrong.

They were not a melody but an ominous song.

I am sorry for what they did to you,

But that bane was eager only for a few.

It consumed and absorbed all the dark,

But you were radiant, with eyes that spark.

The person I met was a gloomy soul,

Spiralling in meaninglessness, her meaningful goal.

But then she rose to the skies above the ground,

She is both the lost and the found.

For she's Shakti, destined to find her Shiva on her own,

And I must submit to the path she has shown.

But I am a poet, and I will never accept

My reality over dreams—

And my poems will be a call for the gods,

The prayers, my screams.

If, for once in this life,

It is possible to meet her in a different form...

I Have the Authority to Say No!

Please don't write to me, for you make this conversation a place where I dwell—in the moment, in the past, and in the time I crave for.

For you make me believe that there is love, and so do I. We are making fools of each other. We are characters of the same story, where we both love passionately and yet love none—as if it's not a serious business, it's only for fun.

So, I do love, and you love one. You keep making me believe that I love one who, except for you, there are none.

All of Life Came at Once

All my heart wrenches with thirst,

All of life came at once,

The surreal thoughts of neither nor,

The question—what am I living for?

A life full of scathes and lies,

And they say life, like all, justifies.

Who will read the mourning shuns?

All the life I lived—I lived all at once.

Body rots, aghast in pain,

And you say blood pitches a vein.

I breathe her tormenting silence,

And I still have to watch through a poetic lens.

The life that was never meant for once,

All of life came at once,

And all my heart wrenches with thirst,

And I can only call it a poetic outburst.

Oh, Life!

Oh life
Put me to death and end me with a knife
O life,
Night has only began with its endless tyranny
And I am a bee collecting misfortunes and not honey,
O life,
End my never ending strife,
Put me to death and end me with a knife

Death has always been my beautiful mistress,
With so much to give and with no distress,
She also presented me a beautiful knife,
Said, "you can forever be with me away from your ugly life".
It's true that you are such a ugly faced, my life.
I have forcefully married with you, with a constant strife.
Death is beautiful and a pause,
But unfortunately you are my truth and cause,
I shall always seek you,
Even if I don't want to,
For you love me more than death,
If death would have loved me she would have taken my breath,

But she always turned me down,
And you, you always made me laugh as if you and I both
are clown,
O life....I shall forever seek you even if I loved death more
than you…

The Idea of You

I want to regret being in love with the idea of you, for that guilt will turn to pride in my poetry, that pain will turn to pleasure, and you will turn into me within my verses.

It has always been worth the wait, for you are always standing—to say hellos and to wave goodbyes.
And the world will gift you with ever-coming "hi"s and never-leaving goodbyes. You will always be there, like death, time, and life itself.

And after ages, poets will sing of your glory—that you were the last man standing on the battlefield, unafraid and unyielding.

It has always been worth the wait.

Love, I Can't Love You More

Love, I can't love you more.

It was yesterday's tale that we were in the middle of the love sea,

a luminant tapestry, and today? We are on shore.

Only the ruined loved the beauty; and now it's only a lore.

Love, I can't love you more.

I have tried a thousandfold To do what they say: clasp and hold,

Like the remnants of your hair strand along the sea breeze—the moment fleeting, yet longing to freeze.

What is unbearable to me and what I have never told you, love.

Love, I can't love you more.

I have always been in what they say is a pitfall.

An image of surreal suffering drawn upon my heart's wall I thus seek only two moments of love, not four Love, I can't love you more.

We were never so close and yet not apart, And in our story, destiny has its part.

Love has despised a lot in me, always fleeting and free.

You know, I can't even stand my ground, For you are always lost and found.

Love never offered me the earth or the sky's floor.

Love, I can't love you more. But even if stories are meant to be incomplete, there is so much to explore.

Perhaps the poet finally begged the Lord to help his love, his story restore, But the Almighty denied what he implored.

His tears shed down, and the Lord spoke to him: "Love, I can't love you more.

Even if you are in a sea of surrender, I command you to come on shore.

Love, I can't love you more."

Is There Any Medication for Belief?

There is no medication for belief.

There is no cure for fanatic devotion.

When the body agrees to the soul in pursuit of self, it laments itself in the forge of suffering. My illness, my hesitation to eat, my eyes are witness of such creation therefore I am creating self. My belief can't be medically tested, my devotion can't be cured.

Your Lordship,

When I was in first year of college, I thought of her, I wished that she should be like fundamental right under the constitution. If she would have been my fundamental right, no one could have abused my right, no one could have taken her away from me. But there was no such right present.

Now, Your Lordship, it came to my knowledge that I have the Right to conscience, and by all heart and the will of the Lord himself, she is the centre of my belief and if there is any rule of law, no one can take my right to bow down to her, to worship her...not even she can take that right away from me. If she does, it is hurting my religious sentiments.

There is no cure for my illness, let me go...

I Plead Guilty

I am guilty of murdering a story for I have not taken a stand for it, for I have not protected it. Rather I became only a Intelligence and not the consciousness. As an intelligence I intelligently choose not to speak, when my conscience and conscious was telling me to do so, and yet I chose to use my intelligence in the most fool way possible.

The crime is done and I am in the dock. And soon when the trial will be over I will be convicted of all my misdeeds in all glory's court, and I shall be devoured for my very own existence. For I am sinful as I exist but in the time of unearthly plight and an uncheering sight, he who holds me, never pulled back his blessing hands upon me. I demand to all whose Lord feels that they are his children to not strangle me but to hit in my heart, to cut and crush every part of mine but let me speak, let me speak to my death, till my death. For when I am silent, I cease to exist.

Alas, What Have You Done?

Page by page, branch by branch,

You poured your soul, you took the chance,

You read every book, every stance.

Yet hunger put you to sleep at night,

Alas, what have you done in your plight?

Begged for mercy, yet couldn't refrain,

Tried every trick, but all in vain.

She stood by you, her loyalty tight,

Yet you wrote her life like a fool outright.

You were a sinner, now a stray,

Alas, what have you done today?

Ha-ha! I've written it all,

Ha-ha! I've penned my fall.

You never once thought of her heart,

The one who made you her friend from the start.

Yet you failed to see, failed to understand,

And held onto her with a desperate hand.

Time asked you to let her go,

Yet you wrote her fate as your own woe.

It's all your fault, admit it now,

Oh, great writer, take a bow!

You have tasted the bitter bread of defeat,

Ha-ha! I've written it all, so sweet.
For once, listen, heed my call,
Oh, great writer, after all.
She was your guide, yet you lost your way,
Alas, what have you written today?
Alas, what have you done today?

The World Has Lit Up for Me

You know, today the world has lit up for me.

I saw squirrels teasing the trees, laughing; the tree was a little annoyed at their mischief, but then it laughed too. The leaves curled up and joined in with their chuckles. Light hid within the shimmering leaves, just like little children hide after playing a prank. I felt happy, seeing the green light smile between the leaves. I even saw the buds blooming.

Life shone so brightly today that I saw old children chatting merrily on the rainbow-colored sands of life. And life itself paused to watch them laugh, just as elders pause to watch children play.

Today, in my attempt to stop time, my slowly beating heart found its rhythm again. It began to beat in tune with life once more.

Autumn has passed now, and spring has arrived. I am moving forward, writing a new world for myself, filled with the grandeur of hope.

Last night, I forgave myself. I sat down with my past and signed a peace treaty.

Today, the world has lit up for me.

NATURE & METAPHORS: WHISPERS OF THE EARTH

Fate of Dandelions

I've lived with Dandelions by the shore,

And the deliquescent fireflies grovelled upto my eyes.

Distant in the forest shade somewhere,

Heard the siren of ambulance gust away.

Yet my hands, as pristine and serene, as the moonlight beam,

Pave the way to the glare of beryl emerald.

As if, to feel is to believe, and live like the last.

As if the stone would sense the trace of my prints.

But the naïve queen gets crushed and promises cut with
paper,

The place reeks of hopelessness.

So when the fireflies are dead and sun feeds upon ocean,

The morning has risen.

Eyes then glued to colossal structures of Delhi.

I woke up and recollect, I've held myself to forces.

In the murk, the demons might have sucked my soul,

But in my wilderness, I streamed love upon them.

And

When fall departed, universe hushed, every little Lily Blossom shall bloom.

The echoes of young bits of tense, blended in my life,

The gloom evanesced into thin air.

The heavens, as charming as mirth, wrapped me in their embrace.

Once more, I danced on my toes, belly ached of laughter.

I watered the smallest ecosystem at hand-me

and I shone like the sound of bliss.

Life Once Struck

Life once struck the yearning sky,
That kept longing for earth, its life, and love.
The sky kept showering rains, and once it reached its low.
The same sky was heaven to the dwellers of earth,
For they never knew their own and the sky's worth.

The sky was peace for the children at war,
And it longed for the life that fought for more.
The sky was infinity of love for lovers on earth,
They thought that love, like the sky, is infinite in worth.
But the sky grew jealous of the zealous and free kite,
Who soared without care, in the vast expanse of light.

On earth, they made a phrase, "Be free as the sky,"
But the sky knew that we are here to say goodbye.
Then, there are many who see the sky, but know only a few,
And there are sailors who know the constellations, and for
them, it's nothing new.

And you know the yearning, the longing of the sky is true—
It is true… it is true.

The Lonely Poet and the Cat

The lonely poet started walking down a street,
With a mind full of thoughts, with a walk discreet.
He saw a cat and then thought,
The cat came near him, and he feared her a lot.

He started walking fast,
She followed him, and he, aghast,
He said, "Don't come near me, O cat,
I am not a good person."

But to her, on the lonely street, he was the only one.
She came near him with her sweet meow,
Which to his dismay, he shouted at her, "Leave me now."
That lovely cat fondled him with her usual gaze,
He flicked her, like the sun flicks haze.

But he was no sun, to be true,
A darkness consumes him, and he asks that question, "Are you?"
The cat, she doesn't care about the poet or his attitude,
Neither his ideas nor his solitude.

The poet flicked her, but she grabbed him with all her strength,
As if the sun is diving, grabbing its own length.
And like all stories, the poet kept the cat,
To keep all his stories to himself, to have an endless chat.

Law and Files

Here most files are crimson red, all lives lost, all dead,

Some files are green and few blue,

What I learnt today is who filed a case against who.

Law is a heap of file,

Seeing it you lose your smile,

Here they say,

Every fact is true,

What I learnt today is who filed a case against who,

Further,

From grave to cheap, here is dense thick heap,

What you sow is not what you reap,

I have files to arrange and have to pass them through,

What I learnt today is who filed a case against who.

It's not what all I learnt,

In some situations you just nod and lowly grunt,

Then you just accept and say, it's not only you,

There are more cases to arrange for a who against who.

Well it's not all true that

I only learnt who filed a case against who

There are types to it,

From summary suit to a Darkhast, Much of proceedings so slow and some so fast,

Much like W.H. Auden law like love,

Law is something that everyone owe,

I have also learnt to use some website, To find the relevant provision and if I have a right,

Sometimes I think I will sit on a heap, Then after a moment I fall from a height,

They say, there is remedy when there is right,

But law is all black and not a bit white,

I have learnt something more than who filed a case against who,

To just nod and accept everything is true,

It is not absolutely about you, law.

Her Words Sharp as Law

Her words are sharp as law on the edge of a sword,

Only who obey them are worthy of reward,

Natural law governs all,

But hers is the positive law that stands tall,

Society is regulated by her order,

Or with law everything will be chaotic, a silent blur.

Only a Few Know It

There are many who see the sky, but only a few know it.

The same sky that shelters war-torn children, with delights of white and wide—stars and galaxies, a cosmos full of possibilities.

The lovers, under the same sky, enjoy the heaven of peace, a world full of hope, and future responsibilities.

The same sky yearns in longing for the earth,
And fades and illuminates in its unworth.

Then the same sky falls on some, taken aback in time, with turmoil that strikes the heart and bends life into a coil.

You know, catastrophe is not for the sky, but only for me and you.
And there are sailors who know the constellations in the sky, and for them, it's nothing new.

Echoing Laugh

Once, a laugh echoed through a thousand spirals,
engulfing all the silence that mourned the longing of hearts.
And my heart surrendered to that laugh,
a laugh both almost recognizable and yet utterly unfamiliar.
Poets, do you know of that laugh?
I seek an answer for it,
I seek that voice again...
the laugh beyond immeasurable pain,
the existence and its bane.
Can you laugh like that?

Abyss of Winter

I have fallen into the abyss of winter,

Where meadows scream, and leaves rattle in perplexing
perpetuity.

My nose, too, runs down in windy fashion,

And I, too, cough and cough all the temporal heroism

That life battered with pain and suffering.

No season has provided me with the handkerchief of company,

Friendship, and trust.

I have survived all seasons, longing for the winter to come

And take me to the abyss,

Where my nose runs down,

And I laugh that I had the same cough from all seasons.

It stayed with me, like the long winter in my heart,

Waiting for a summer to come,

Taking me to the shores of the sun,

The warmth of life,

The cure for my cold of loneliness.

The Unwritten Just

The monsoon came, sweeping all the bane on earth's monsoon flower. Rain fell upon it as a shower. It felt as if the monsoon flower was bathing in the bloom of monsoon, enjoying every word of rain, giving up on her tantrums and pain. The world seemed so serene and just, for the monsoon had arrived, washing away the rust.

Then, the monsoon flower whispered, *"I don't want you to leave me."*

The monsoon felt joyous and free; it rose in cheerfulness and fell into the dawning depths of the earth.

Yet, in that joy, it found itself losing its worth.

The monsoon flower hesitated and asked, *"What if my lover, my sun, returns?"*

The monsoon, smiling, replied, *"I will let myself burn for you."*

But the monsoon flower didn't want that either. *"Please go back,"* she pleaded.

"I don't want such a consequence for you."

The monsoon, a true friend to the earth, wished to stay,
forgetting its own worth.

It poured down with all its love for a few days,

But soon, the sun began its ascent with shining rays.

The monsoon flower, torn between past and present, lifted
an umbrella,

Pushing the monsoon away—

The only way to save her heart.

And so, the monsoon gloomed.

Now, when it rains, it is nothing but tears of longing for her—

For his once dear friend,

For whom the monsoon once wrote the rain.

PHILOSOPHY & SOCIETY:
THE MIND'S BATTLEFIELD

War is Peace

And they asked the poet, of war
and he said,
"Of war, I only know one thing,
who says that war is for peace?
they are betrayers of mankind,
there is no war where peace you can find,
War is the creation of a conflicting mind,
where love sparks it and hate drives,
when the brain becomes deaf and the heart turns blind,
what man searches in it and for what he strives.
for sure,
war is a hopeless romance,
a game of death and not of chance.
Man is at constant war on both sides,
it's in his heart where peace resides.
but he won't dare to look inside,
Hate is to show and love is to hide.
hmmm......
I haven't witnessed a victory in arms,
but I had been bewitched by someone's charms."
The poet spoke of his muse,
everyone surrounded him in shocking amuse.
he spoke,

"there I saw a girl with curls,
hairs brown and eyes as pearls.
Unlike barbarians of rage, she stood calm,
A quiet beauty, a greater weapon of harm.
She had a unique sword as if not a sword but a pen,
Owing to her appearance, anyone can misread,
I witnessed her chopping dozens of head,
Truly whatever her sword was, her spirit was insane.
and thus, I was taken as a prisoner of war."
and "then what happened O poet?", one of the folks asked
and he said,
"of them all, they spared me,
to tell a story,
of man's misdeeds and his non-sense glory."
"What happened to her, that girl?"
"hmmm.... that girl"
"I plead them to set me free"
and she replied,
"A poet writing for me, there is no way I can set him free."
"I am still a prisoner
a day-walking dreamer.....
and that too is a war.....
For war is not for peace,
there is only war, war amidst
For war is only in the mind
and it is there peace you can find."

Political, Social and Moral Obscenity

Today I woke up with a strange dream,

Where I was buying onion and garlic with political supreme.

I questioned the oppressive taxes on the masses,

They silenced me with promise of Jashn e Rekhta's premium passes.

As a corrupted poet of heart and soul, politics is not my holy goal,

Neither I am interested in the morals of the poet and his societal role.

So today I woke up really early, so early that even the sun was shocked.

As if a right question to a right answer in KBC is locked.

It was for a much-awaited tea,

With a muse and a face pretty.

I skipped all the morning chores,

To sail on uncharted shores,

Rushed there with unimaginable flight,

With back in mind that I am an idiot, this isn't right.

Within 25 minutes or so I reached there much early,

With radiant glow.

I was 20 km from my home you know, and as always, she was late.

Ah and I had to do something for it is permanent wait.

How can one spend the timeless time, waiting is not poetry, it is straight it doesn't have to rhyme.

So, I called my cousin telling him of my observations on lust and love,

Telling him that sometimes you have to be carnal and kill love's divine dove.

How you can be creep for being honest and sense,

Only my heart knew the pain of waiting in my veins.

So, I told him that even if the discussion has been for thousands of years,

Man has never been true to himself out of his primal fears.

Meanwhile she texted an apology for being late,

It was another 10 minutes of wait.

Even that philosophical discussion ended soon,

And I was admiring the morning moon.

Then she came after 20 minutes, with stole on her face,

And riding her scotty in surreal race.

She stopped and said, "I am really sorry for being late, I am just so so sorry."

I so wanted to tell her, dearest, my heart has already stopped it is not in hurry.

She is my muse, I only have to speak of her beauty,

Her eyes sharp and presence witty.

A smile as dart and a with a poet's mysterious heart.

But to common folks, she is the woman with whom you can imagine all sins,

Don't think that way, she will just hold her prejudice strong, it will be her win.

After all, to her all men are the same,

It is not love that drives, its carnal game.

To be true for her I never had those lewd desires,

its her mystery that I respire.

We started walking towards a walking lane,

Where we started talking on the issues of existence and bane.

I told her about my experiments of permanent admiration,

She told me that, it doesn't workout much, its like vacation.

She just laughed in her own smarter way and said, you know everything is just ephemeral thing,

I prefer the spark of bodies, it's better to fling.

Fling? I have heard it before, I know the literal meaning for the sure, but I was still new for me,

Who will think of bodies to be taken as bodies, lustful, so full of passion and that free?

It was new thought for my Brain to process,

Much like the GST after the cess.

I was listening to her as a devotee listen to a Saint's sermons,

To take their own interpretation of divinity that reach nothingness, no ones.

She was of the view that love is only a veil for lust,

That to be avoidant of it is hypocritic and unjust.

It doesn't mean that fling is only passion and heat,

I told her, we should first find a seat.

Yes, we were at different place now, where just two strangers talk,

It was necessarily essential after a walk.

Then we talked of kisses, and how I didn't feel a thing,

She told me that's the reason I just fling.

Only God knows this time, that my eyes were not only in her eyes a plain,

I was watching her turbulent voluptuous body too,

And I knew that her touch could make me insane.

I thought of it all this time,

We discussed Nabokov too, and his poetic chime,

This attraction I felt apart from poetry was surreal and sublime.

They were waves of sleep, sleep that could make me imagine,

That this time I am on cloud and heaven and in front of her on bottom nine.

If it is just for the sake of spark, I felt that with her I could intertwine.

As they say one in passion above and below,

Let your senses blur in faith, let your body flow.

This time it was not the itch of the creation, but poetic passion,

That was screaming hard, muse, with you today I want to be one.

My hands were telling me to hold her as if she is mine,

To hold her down from waist making everything there in unrest.

I wanted to feel the kiss as she told me at its best.

I was so drowning in it that like a pervert I wanted to take you behind the bush,

Where you resisted first and then lingered shush.

It was attraction, the real pull and push.

It felt almost real,

Where we were at the same area where a guard was attacked by a leopard's cub,

And we made the whole of the jungle a carnal playground, our personal bath tube.

The whole of it was surrounded with ecstasy and the roar of pleasure,

Again, we talked and laughed beyond measure.

The imagination ended with the last sip of coffee,

For every sip has its tale.

And in the end, you told me, you are 6'2 why don't you fling a few,

I had my reasons you know…

For I wanted the tryst with destiny once,

As Life wanted permeance with ephemerality and all it got was ephemerality with permeance.

Well, you asked for the work if I have written too

And I am still at the question how could I and you?

Well I thought of it….should I really send this one too?

A Poet in the Crowd

A Poet stood his ground firm and in the market of wanderers and seekers he sang his poems out loud and all alone. Numerous passersby crossed his road, some heard him in delight, some called him a madman and some were astonished by his resolve to be just there all alone and calling. One fine night, God asked him, "Till when are you going to be here? No one is listening to you; you are just wasting what I have given you. This suffering, this pain, everything I have created is useless, it has no meaning to it."

" Lord, this uselessness, this despair, this misery, this search of mine everything is so meaningful for me for I know that my poetry is reading me, for I know that I will have to wait to meet her somewhere else, some other time, in some other costume and I will wait until my poetry completes."

"What if your poetry leaves you, what if you are not read, you are not seen and all of it is meaningless."

"I will still abide by it, it's my destiny to align with the stories and let them defy my faith."

God stared at him in astonishment and laughed, "What a madman!"

Destiny of the Bridge

I laughed at my own hopeless that like a bridge I am destined to witness my muse, the river flowing through time, she is destined to meet the sea and only in my own destruction I can meet her. But everyone keeps repairing me for their own purpose and I keep living and suffering.

Everyone is In

Everyone is in love, everyone has some pain,
That's what happen when we use our hearts and not the brain

Their eyes are filled with joy and to tears they call rain,
That's what happen when

They call everyone the last and laugh, and says it happened again,
That's what happen when

Every time when they failed to express, they took up a pen,
That's what happen when

They are held, captivated and they merrily show their wound
say it's from love of chain,
That's what happen when

Do People Care?

How terribly idiot he was to believe that people do care and
soon everything was a felony, a betrayal, a despair. Think
of a sane mind, yours and my kind, a believer who turned
blind of his own reckless beliefs so unwind. How terrible
it is to believe that something exists and then finding that
something to be nothing

No One Will Understand!

No one will ever understand, how it is to be lonely at nights,
As if you are all alone in the war for your rights,
The constitution of God never guaranteed that you will meet
your human self,
Nor it stated that you will get any help,
Still you believed in him, his Dynasty of peace and prosperity,
And yet he is nowhere to pity,
No one will ever understand,
To have utmost faith in his creation of righteousness, beauty
and joy,
And have all your dreams ransacked as troy,
No one will ever understand the laughter and mockery of
nights,
When you are all alone amidst the chaos and your long fights,
No one will, no one,
And when the similar curse will fall thundering upon you,
I will clap the bolts and start my revolt against his kingdom of
hope, devouring hope,
For no one has ever understood, no one has

Source of My Faith

"Oh, holiness, your eyes are the source of all my faith. As if I have never prayed to anyone but you. All the prayers I have sung so fervently were and are in devotion to you, not Him. I am the greatest sinner on this dying land, yet I offer roses to the merriest of them all—you. Your eyes are the cathedral to a soul that confesses its sins there. My soul has seen you in place of the Lord himself, and in its piety, it loves you, not God. As your pious devotee, I wish that you may always look upon me with your kind, loving, and caring eyes, and I will always gaze upon you as if a mere human is looking towards the radiant sun."

Even a Life is Not Enough

Even a life is not enough to talk about you, to speak through your heart, to make you understand what lies beyond the words...not even a life, lives are not enough and only in one of billionth of billion possibilities I can hold your hand, speak about you to you only and in that possibility it will be finally possible to read you all the poems that I have written for you.

POETRY ON POETRY:
THE POET'S SOUL

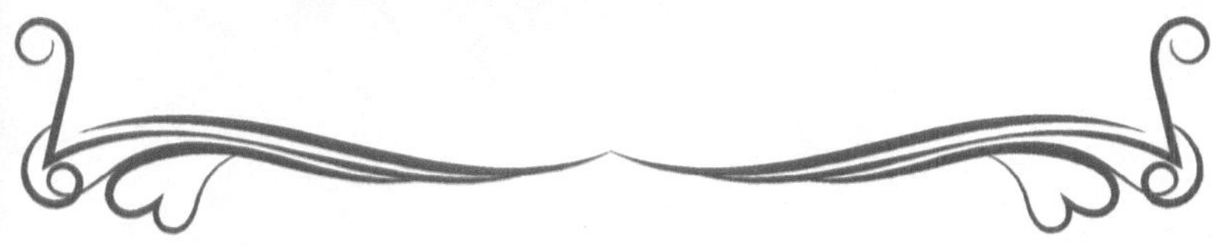

What Poetry Does to You

Poetry compels you to love, it make you hate,
It forces you to let go, it makes you wait,
Then at the end, you pen it all down and call it fate.

Poem Without a Rhyme

The stars gazed upon the night,
While poems lingered, waiting for rhyme.
Questions searched for answers,
Efforts faded, lost in time.

And my friend, sometimes, I stay silent—
For every good reason, you know...
Yet in the end, silence itself
Spoke of the need to talk.

Silence Has Turned Stranger to Me Today

Silence has turned stranger to me. She no longer speaks, nor looks at me with the same elegant admiration. Whenever, I look at her with my same longing and urge for conversation, she turns her face. I have never seen silence as silent like this, why? I don't know, she is no longer a voice in my head, capable of creating a protruding chaos, nor she is chaos herself. Silence is slowing becoming a void, emptiness that is devouring me with all it's nothingness. I am talking more for I am becoming more silent, I am turning a stranger to myself. I fear if I start talking out aloud all my voice will be taken and I will be left empty, empty as silence is becoming now.

Muse

A talk with the muse is a poet's feast,

But for it he kept waiting and stared at a ticking clock on his wrist.

While waiting he thought about all the injustices done to him, by the muse he loved and whim.

At some point he thought of letting go, only to stop for a latent snow.

He thought of other things too,

Meagre to him but significant to you.

He thought of people of faith waiting long in a cruel queue, then he thought of children of war, what the world pledge for them and leader's snore.

He thinks of all while waiting in uncertainty, for a beloved he admires, for a face too pretty. But then in waiting and absence he thinks of all ugliness in the world, rotten and dead's, blinded and misleads... even waiting for a muse is good you know...who knows what idea lord will throw.

Ah...I will tell you my story some other day, you know I am waiting for a feast. Let me check what time is it.

But there was no watch on the poet's wrist.

What a man!

A Poet's Refuge

A poet sought refuge in your solace arms,

Even he could not refuse your serene charms,

For your soul is more divine than his art,

You soothe him and his heart,

He is forever grateful to you

He wants to kiss your writings palms,

touch your feet and bow down to your wits,

For you are greater than all his tricks,

And your silence is stronger than what he speaks.

The Affection

O wordily soul of eastern bay,

You lay claim on the poet's way,

Sometimes so attentive and sometimes so distractive,

How can one be so fine in words and in demeanour so active

The Curiosity

It's your language that makes me speak,

And I get filled up with all word's curiosity
to know it better.

I take my chances with open arms, but you are well
protected by charms.

I do want to write something for you,

But what can I create a new.

You have already a wisdom of the old,

And beauty of the dawn to light and unfold. I can't impress
you with words miss Poet, you own them already.

Wonder in Your Eyes

I see the wonder setting in your eyes, vibrant and flamboyant in nature and you are staring at it as if all night shifts to the nuances of hope and plight. I am just a watch keeper who wants to adorn you with time, and gift you the eternality of rhymes.